gentle freedom,
gentle courage

Much love
Much happiness
And a gentle heart.
        Fondest Love
          Edna.

Other books by

Blue Mountain Press INC.

gentle freedom, gentle courage

poems on friendship, love and life, including
the poem "a friend so rare"

diane
westlake

♔
Blue Mountain Press ™.
Boulder, Colorado

ISBN: 0-88396-079-6
Library of Congress Number: 80-65753

Manufactured in the United States of America
First Printing: March, 1980
Second Printing: September, 1980

Acknowledgments:
Thanks to Blue Mountain Arts creative staff, with special thanks to
Douglas Pagels and Cliff Scott.

We gratefully acknowledge the permission granted by the author to
reprint the following previously copyrighted poems in this publication:

a friend so rare, beyond my window, we can go, we must remain,
allow me to live, each of us, whatever the struggle, joy of love, we
touch, wind brings sounds, my hands, new love soars, you possess,
blue your swift cycle, i am free, you are free, whatever it is, don't
mistake, keep in mind; Copyright © Diane Westlake, 1977. All rights
reserved.

Blue Mountain Press INC.

P.O. Box 4549, Boulder, Colorado 80306

Contents

dedication

to those with the champion's heart
from which flows
pure unconditional love

introduction

a friend told me, recently, after reading my books, that she felt i had written not only for her, but, that i had written to her . . . that was, for me, a most important evaluation of my work . . . for there are those things . . . i have written into the words . . . which are more than the words i have written on the paper . . . those things i have written to you.

it is my desire and intent to bring, to each of you, whatever message, solace, guidance, affirmation, courage or joy you seek at the times that you read my writings . . . and, it is my desire and intent, always, to bring, to you, my love and blessings through my words.

Diane Westlake

a friend so rare
you stand by me no matter what
the good or bad of my life . . .

you never disappoint me
when i need to depend on your support
you tell me when i am wrong
so gently you guide me without pain
you love me even when we disagree

each day and night
   i feel your presence
you may not be near to touch
but you are in my mind and heart
you meet my needs so silently
i am not alone because of you . . .

whatever i am that causes you
to love me with this loyalty . . . i pray
that i am as much for you
as you are for me
my friend i love you

beyond my window
the world waits
you are there
my source . . . my ending
my vessel overflowing
with possibilities
of all our beginnings

it was . . . because of you
and because of you . . . it is now
that life has opened before me
strengths i never had
are mine to use and share
joy so often out of reach
surrounds and fills me
i do not need to see you
            (though i see you in my heart)
for peace to rise softly from the earth
through the length of me
creating inside my head . . . a fluid calm
sending out from my body
a love so strong for everyone
it heals as it circles . . . and encircles
returning to me to hold or use again
or carry with me throughout life
and all of this is mine
because of you

Constant companion
light of my days and nights
you are loyalty and love
asking nothing . . . giving all
my heart is full
for you have filled it

The friends who count
pull you from your aloneness
when you are not certain
you want to come from there
who hold you at the time you think
you do not want to be touched
they are the ones who fill your bowl
with warm and wholesome food
though your emotion has lost
your body's appetite
those friends who count
are the ones in the chair
beside your bed
as you wake in the morning
of the night you cried
yourself to sleep
then laugh with you
in the sun of a new today

We can go
as far as
love and sharing
will take us

We must remain open for the feeling of love
vibrations between hearts and minds
giving each other our silences
giving each other our deeds
leaving each one to his peace and solitude

allow me to live my life as i choose
according to the way i think
following my mind
accepting others as i see them
do not judge me by your standards
for we have traveled different roads
which have brought us to this point of meeting
we know different truths
we do not feel the same
yet i can love you
respect the total which is you
especially because you are fully unique
as am i
remember . . . though . . . love and respect
are sustained only if you do not try
    to change me
nor i you
the excitement of life lies in expectations
of the differences we may share tomorrow
be yourself
i'll be me
the world is open
to touch everyone we meet
freely

each of us may
do or say
those things
which our integrity
dictates
but we must be prepared
at all times
to face and accept
responsibility and consequence
for our own actions

In all you do
you must come forth
from that place of honor
within yourself
then . . . hold true
being honorable
in every interaction
of your life

you cannot take the lesson
to the pupil
the pupil must come
to the lesson

your gentle heart shows itself to me
as you learn your lessons
one by one . . . open already for the next
your eyes are clear . . . mind alert
and i watch you grow
you are the treasure that you seek
but you do not know that yet
for the months and years ahead
are yours to fill with gains and losses
i see you now as i saw you then
go forward gallant and eager pupil
carry your light with equal pride and humility
you are your own reward
a gift so great to the people
of the universe . . . your energy flows in circles
conduct . . . channel . . . reach to the highest
it is yours for eternity

There is a place so high
you think you cannot reach there
it is the place where you have always seen
your heroes . . . the ones you enthroned there
there is a place so strong
within you which has not been used . . .
if you give it power
you will rise up . . . easily
to stand beside the magnificence
of the ones you dared not touch
reach down now
activate the glory that is you
stand atop the high place that is yours

Whatever the struggle
continue the climb
it may be only
one step to the summit

You are equal to all others
some may have greater talents and power
where you are lacking
but you are greater in areas
    where they cannot go
do not stop your own growth and progression
by trying to emulate . . . or follow . . . anyone
step out with courage
develop all that you are meant to be
look for new experiences . . .
    meet new people

learn to add all new dimensions
to your present and future
you are one of a kind . . .
        equal to every other person
accept that fact
live it   use it   stand tall
in belief of who you are
reach for the highest accomplishment
touch it   grasp it
know it is within your ability
live to win in life
and you will

Power
  strength and self assertion
lie within us all
yet we are afraid
we do not use the resources
given to us to lift our lives
from the stagnation of comfortable routine
locked into jobs, relationships . . . ourselves
fearing what others may think of us
we lack the courage to step
        from our accustomed role
strength and self assertion
        can be demonstrated
with gracious kindness
softly spoken truths will take us farther
than belligerent defensiveness
be true to yourself . . . dare to be different
by courageously stepping forward
to say "i am" . . . "i will be"
then "be"
remembering always to move softly
with gentleness and love
free yourself from what others want you to be
that with which you have aligned yourself
find and use the magnificent
loving power within you

Vastness of the world around
simplicity of the heart within
love can easily encircle
the universe with calming, cherishing
beams of light . . . so smoothly and gently
it touches the deepest part of another's soul
that corner most protected one day opens
under constant caresses of a loving spirit
in that moment the protector wonders
how it was that no one . . . before . . .
        cared enough
to stay so long . . . love so deeply . . .
        wait so patiently
for the warming away of the coldness
        of a heart
this long hidden
now . . . intensity of the love felt
soft tenderness of the offering
        meets no resistance
love merely enters in and surrounds
now . . . simplicity within two hearts
peace of the loving together

joy of love
to share two lives as one
giving unending
received
to turn
and
give again

We touch
in all life around us
remaining together in space
we have shared
your breath soft on my cheek
imprints of you forever
in my heart

Wind brings sounds
of your laughter over the earth
filling the space of eternity
i touch you always
for you are of my flesh
you are in my soul

my hands are for you
to give you all i can of what you need
play a melody to ease your trouble
lift you when you have exhausted your strength
arouse the soft responsive places of your body
lay across your shoulders in warm comradeship
soothe your brow as you require comfort
guide you when you have lost your way
place on your knee as we sit in friendship
hold your hands in pleasure and in joy
reach out in our greetings and farewells
touch you with love my friend
please
take my hands
they are for you

New love soars bringing courage and light hearted joy
everything is possible . . . each moment apart is emptiness
the world looks like your lover . . . desire consumes
togetherness brings the truth that two are one
each one's thought is as the other's simultaneous discovery
wholeness of person replaces life's incompleteness
time passes and feelings settle to comfortable security
understanding the need to give time and patience
always a bit of yourself . . . compromise
with no loss of identity . . . both of you
giving and receiving rising above insignificant faults
the thread of love weaves life's patterns everchanging
each of you grows and moves in new directions
giving tender care to your times together
unique individuals sharing what you are
two special beings . . . you are each other

If you have one friend who loves you
you are protected
safe from the world and your fears within . . .
whatever you say or do from your conviction
will pass from you . . . perhaps returning . . .
even though you hurt now
with pain suffered from the efforts
your heart may retreat
into the love and tolerance
of the friend who takes you as you are

the one who sees your faults
and loves you for them
who knows your virtuous strengths
and grows from accepting your total person
just as you grow and are protected
by the sharing of the love
which flows between the two of you . . .
as you return that love
you become the one friend
of the friend who loves you

the pleasures and pains
which arise inside of us
when thinking on loving
are constant in life
no one goes untouched by sexuality
affected somewhere from tightly closed
to full flower open
fulfilled loving
brings a beautiful ecstasy
no loving at all
is quiet desolation . . .
acutely felt . . .
between the two
the line so fine
stretches from birth to death
and the learning in the middle
causes all life to function
from beginning to end
loving arches its power
commanding us all

there is spirituality
in every act and word

there is sexuality
in every act and word

love is . . .
spiritual mental and emotional union
physical closeness is . . .
what you do about it

The moon reflects tonight
our love
fresh from the sun's light today
as ever . . . a sphere of constant warmth
enclosed us in the safe place
of each other's heart
soft hands touching and strong embrace
brought . . . as always . . . steady blending
of our energies . . .
    each within and into the other
locking together our souls and spirits
inseparable for the moment
and upon parting
never apart

i am love
the one who follows even after death
having no beginning no end
you see me in your myriad visions
never seeing me at all . . . yet i am there
everywhere for everyone . . . ever in and around you
no one escapes my sensation
some run to me . . . some from me
at times i am illusive or illusion
but i hover . . . standing near to all
here for you at your discernment
if you know how to have me and you wish it
the secret is . . . to yield . . . let me come for you
i will come most often in another person
family . . friend . . lover . . man or woman
it does not matter . . . you will find me
in a spectrum of degrees of intensity
and the form of every expression
you will feel me in the center of your body
spreading over you to give you strength
or weakness . . . it depends on how i touch you
and you will find me in the timelessness of space

encompassing the universe in swirls of tenderness
a gentle aching for the joy of discovery
or the pain of loss . . . a gentle aching
for the simple static waiting for me to move you
i am there . . . and i am here . . . i exist
indestructible irreversible ubiquitous
never do i leave you . . . i do not go away
even if the one who brought me to you departs
i am as matter i cannot be destroyed
you use me in many postures . . . or put me deep within
the wisest among you holds me softly inside
always knowing how to offer me to others
and with the offering i grow and surround
your worlds with greater force . . . deeper beauty
even when all of you are gone . . . i remain
i am eons old yet always new if you remember
to reflect on how i feel when i am used correctly
care for me and those you receive in my name
and i will bless each of you with my word
for
i am love

you possess a golden candle in my heart
you with whom i have shared
so many secret and special moments of life

there are rainbows everywhere in life
as the sun touches even particles of dust
color shines through
let the sun light your world
and rainbows surround you
all it costs is time and stillness
give yourself one calm and brilliant moment
today and ever after

even the grey is beauty
folding out above the trees
anointed by rainfall . . .
brown earth turning dark
as it receives nourishment
to set free its buds and grasses
rain brings calm
to the inner man
renewing the knowledge
that god creates all realities
man creates only what he can
he must be ever watchful
to strive to match the manner
of the growing and giving
in god's universe
with the matching . . . then
give forth his own offerings
as he is washed clean
beneath the grey
turning blue lavender and white
                    . . . releasing . . .

blue your swift cycle swings
turns to orange bursting morning
into the room . . . life begins another day
joy replaces sorrows of the night
serenity sets solid and brings the mind
to face ideas . . . counter new experiences
god is here to talk before coffee
begin new day — bring what you will
we'll find ourselves in your bright entrance

living is moving on and up
it is giving in and giving away
the right things at the right time
all it takes is the courage to do it
knowing and believing in the divine timing
of your days
you are new
only when you have released . . .
     totally . . . the old
you must not stay on the same level of being
there always is another way to awareness
grow   change   become
the strength you need deep within
will rise to the surface . . . join consciousness
and bring your transformation
ask for newness
call upon your forces
display your courage
accept the change
believe in your right
to have it

i am free when i know and am myself
  and i allow others that freedom
i am free when i have realized a dream
  and i go forward in new directions
i am free when i choose to follow for love
  and respect . . . but am not controlled by fear

you are free to leave
those things in life
which cause you pain
          once healed
          and in control
          you may return

              you have
              a choice

Whatever it is
learn to live with it
or change it

flexibility is the key to living
nothing is absolute
things that bring you down will pass
and happiness will fill your days
keep yourself open for joys of the heart
lift up your head and laugh at the sky
for someday soon it's certain to be
heaven's going to smile on you

No matter how much
you think . . . know . . . or have learned
never shut your mind
to the thoughts, words and teachings
of others
for there is always a different way
in which to understand and express
a thought or concept
listen to what each person says
use those principles which fit your life
learning must never cease
and self ego should not block
the passage
between ear and mind

When you attain success
retain humility
lest you find your ego
to be greater
than your accomplishment

don't mistake

kindness
gentleness
silence

for weakness

Keep in mind
that each of us is special
because we are different
we have come together
in this friendship
because we have our differences
to bring to each other
so listen to me
as i listen to you
we will hear ourselves
grow into the realization
of expanding mutual respect

for the people in your life . . .

    if you miss them
    tell them
    when you think of them
    let them know

Diane Westlake

"Poets are all who love, who feel great truths,
and tell them; and the truth of truths is love."

Phillip J. Bailey

About the Author

The writings of Diane Westlake reflect a special intuition and positive outlook that are very much a part of her life. Diane is a caring, confident, dedicated individual who reaches out to people with her words and her actions.

A native Californian, Diane grew up along the oceanfront areas of southern California where she fostered an early love for sports, activities and the natural surroundings. She was once very active physically as a teacher in the public schools before becoming crippled with arthritis. But refusing to submit to the handicap, Diane overcame this affliction with time, desire and an association with wholistic healing practices.

Diane now lives in a quaint village on the coast, counseling, teaching, writing and exploring the wonders of the human spirit. She continues to write poetry, as she has for more than 30 years, to capture and communicate her thoughts. The insights shared through her writings are precious ones, serving as a reassurance of self-worth and potential to us all. Diane sees the world — its natural side and its spiritual counterpart — as a wondrous place to be; a world meant for sharing and growing, learning and living life to its fullest.